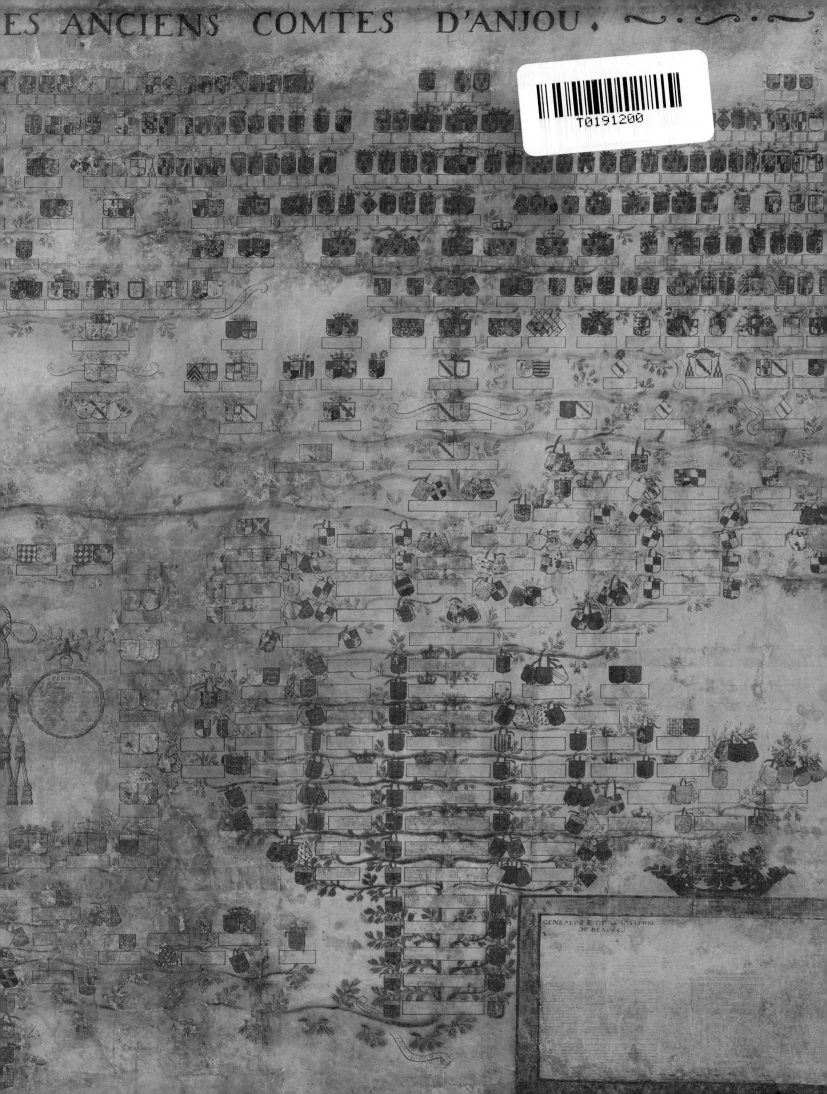

GENEALOGIE DE LA MAISON
DE BEAUÇAY

CHÂTEAU DE HAROUÉ

THE HOME OF THE PRINCES DE BEAUVAU-CRAON

CHÂTEAU DE HAROUÉ

A GREAT FRENCH ESTATE, A FAMILY HOME

Victoria Botana de Beauvau-Craon

PHOTOGRAPHY BY

Miguel Flores-Vianna

TEXTS BY MINNIE DE BEAUVAU-CRAON AND MONIQUE RAUX

CREATIVE DIRECTION BY PETER COPPING

RIZZOLI
NEW YORK

New York · Paris · London · Milan

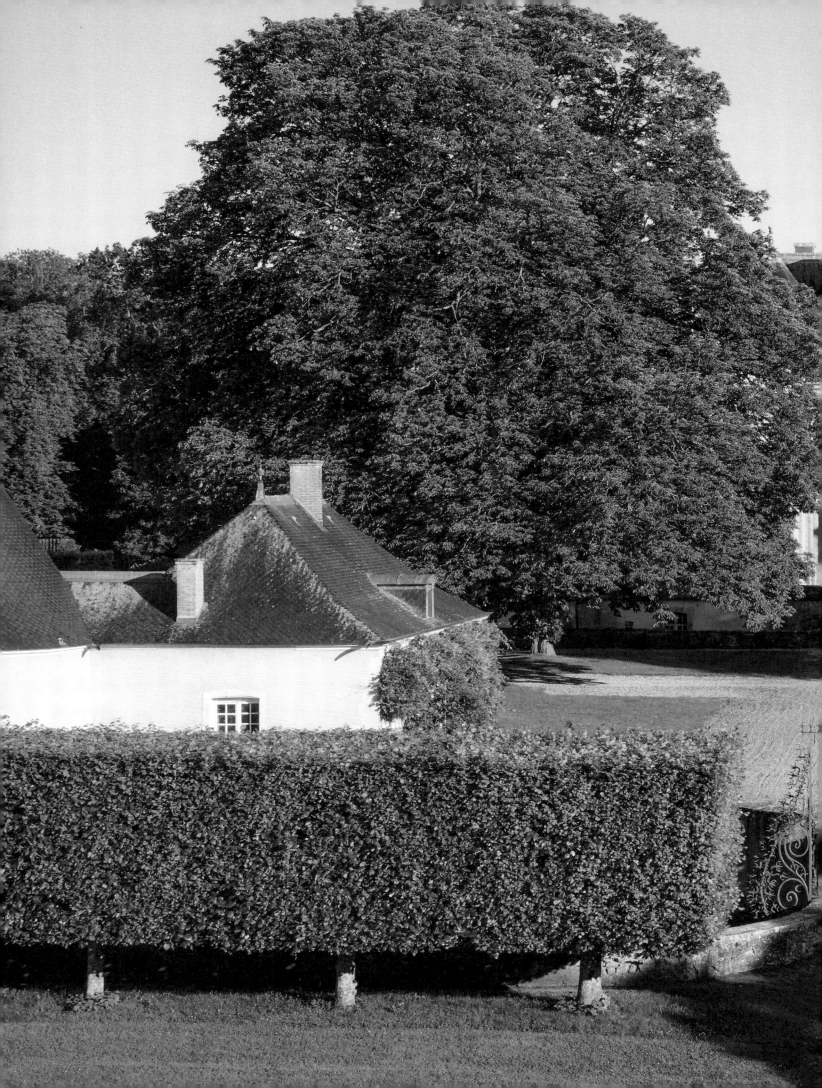

CONTENTS

FOREWORD

JEAN-LOUIS DENIOT

For me, the Beauvau-Craon princes are the epitome of Frenchness. Their motto, *"Sans départir"* ("Never to forsake"), evokes great vision, self-assurance, dependability, untiring intrepidness, and determination.

The Beauvau-Craon lineage dates back to the Byzantine era. The name embodies taste, stability, excellence, and power—a power that comes from their princely approach to life. Through the choices they have made, the Beauvau-Craon family have acquired an ever higher mastery of the French art of living—a way of life that is illustrated by a will to share with others through initiating major commissions that have historically brought together architects, artists, craftspeople, technical experts, historians… and of course the public.

Major commissions are never a matter of selfishness; rather, they are completely collaborative. The Beauvau-Craon family loves to create and build, always seeking to combine functionality with absolute beauty. There is a purity and grandeur to their projects, as if they were drawing closer to the gods. Their major architectural commissions and patronage of French art reflect their powerful political aura. It is thanks to the divine Anne-Marguerite de Ligniville, Princess of Beauvau-Craon and wife of Prince Marc de Beauvau-Craon, that the greatest names in the history of eighteenth-century art worked at the Château de Haroué.

The château's design, by Germain Boffrand, a pupil of Jules Hardouin-Mansart, appears modern for its time. This eighteenth-century palace reflects France at its peak and how it shone on the world stage in the late seventeenth century under King Louis XIV's influence. The Beauvau-Craon princes were great art lovers and collectors of paintings. The 1754 inventory mentions more than four hundred pictures obtained from art lovers' collections by Mignard, Canaletto, Le Sueur, Rembrandt, Poussin, Nattier, and numerous Flemish painters. It was one of the finest collections in France at the time.

Because of its palatial scale, and the harmony and perfect fittingness of its decors, Haroué very quickly made an impression on me and began to influence the evolution and form of my architectural and interior work. I have adored the Beauvau-Craon princesses and princes, as well as Haroué itself, for almost thirty years. Thanks to Diane de Beauvau-Craon, and to Minnie, Victoria, and Sebastian, I have been fortunate enough to have quarters there over many years. In particular, I had the benefit of a studio on the top story of one of the towers, with a view over the garden designed by Emilio Terry, where I had some exciting creative moments and formed some completely magical memories. Since then, I have retained the same taste for large-scale work and grand architectural gestures, and have designed private palaces in India, Russia, Asia, and the United States. The scale of my built projects is similar to that of Haroué—this wonderful palace whose construction required nine years' work and a hundred laborers.

Lavish parties marked the culmination of work at Haroué in a mellow atmosphere of fantasy and mystery. Dinners, masked balls, fireworks, theatrical performances, musical and choral concerts, late-night conversations… all celebrating this unique place at the height of its magnificence. Long may this legacy of major, inclusive, collaborative artistic commissions continue… *Sans départir*!

INTRODUCTION

MINNIE DE BEAUVAU-CRAON

During uncertain times, we all need something to look forward to. In the spring of 2019, during a conversation with my daughter, Victoria, I suggested that we create a beautiful book on our "family home."

We thought a fine-art photographer would offer a fresh perspective on Haroué. Victoria, remarkably efficient as always, got in contact with Miguel Flores-Vianna, an Argentine photographer who lives in London. He immediately shared our enthusiasm and came to visit us at Haroué in July.

Miguel stayed here for twelve days, during which he roamed freely. He explored every corner of the house from its cellars to its attics, absorbing the spirit of Haroué and the quality of its ever-changing light—soft in the evening and brighter in the morning. As much as Victoria and Miguel wanted to show the château's beauty and authenticity, they also wanted to show the unseen.

I was twenty-nine when my father, Marc de Beauvau-Craon, the seventh and last Prince of Beauvau-Craon, suddenly passed away from a heart attack while getting ready to attend Sunday mass in the village church on November 21, 1982. He was sixty-one. At the time, I was living a carefree life in London with Javier, my husband and Victoria and Sebastian's father.

The attachment I now feel to Haroué cannot be explained in any rational way; it is beyond reason. It is not emotional nor is it something quantifiable. It is my life, my soul, and my anchor. This house is a part of me.

Haroué represents far more than an old building steeped in history. It is my roots. In 1982, I had no idea how my life was about to change, how exciting it would become, while still being a challenge every day. I had become a link in a long, unbroken chain; suddenly in charge of taking care of this monument that is part of the Lorraine region's history as well as that of France's.

I wanted to stay faithful to the memory of my father, who was twenty-one when he inherited it in 1942, when his father, Prince Charles-Louis de Beauvau-Craon, passed away. He tackled the château's restoration head on and opened it to the public in 1964. He also got involved in public life to protect the region's interests. He was Mayor of Haroué for twenty-seven years, from 1947 to 1974, and General Councillor of Meurthe-et-Moselle, before becoming President of La Demeure Historique, an association for the preservation of France's historic private stately home owners. He was loved and respected, regardless of whether people knew him as "Monsieur Marc" or as "Prince." As children, my sister, Diane, and I would spend our holidays at Haroué with our nanny, Miss Baker. We would spend our days cycling around the little roads of the rolling countryside, known as the Saintois, with Yen, our boxer dog. In August we would participate with our friends from the village in the picking of the mirabelle plums, which to this day produce the most magical liqueur.

My sister, Diane, is also one of the many pillars of the house. Her elegance, her sense of fun, and her joie de vivre are a refuge and a comfort for me. I often say that we are "light and shadow." I love her.

In 1972, my father married Laure du Temple de Rougemont. She adopted the house and brought with her a breath of fresh air—she became very attached to Haroué. In 1983, after my father's death, Laure became President of Sotheby's France and opened up the French art market to the international auction houses.

One of my first challenges was to give the house even more panache and energy. I thought there was no better way to do this than by creating innovative exhibitions to attract more visitors. Many friends who share our love for Haroué helped us along the way.

The first exhibition, *Les Châteaux disparus du roi Stanislas* (The Lost Châteaux of King Stanisław), with three-dimensional maquettes, was in 1984 followed by *The Unprecedented Boffrand* (Boffrand the Extraordinary) in 1986, both organized with the help of Albert France-Lanord, my very knowledgeable friend who set up the unparalleled Musée du Fer (Iron History Museum) in Nancy as well as Claudine Prouvé, daughter-in-law of the acclaimed architect and designer Jean Prouvé; both are from the Lorraine region. From then on exhibitions became a yearly summer rendez-vous. The themes ranged from Gien, Christofle, and Baccarat to *L'Art de la table* (The Art of Table Settings), with tables set by Alberto Pinto, Kenzo, Isabelle de Borchgrave, Bruno Roy, Hubert de Givenchy, Philippe Venet, and Bunny Mellon; to *Stanislas, duc de Lorraine, roi jardinier* (Stanisław, Duke of Lorraine, Gardener King)…

The success of these exhibitions allowed the theme of friendship to thrive. My dear friends and world-renowned designers Philippe Venet and Hubert de Givenchy created one of the first fashion exhibitions in a stately home with the 2010 exhibition *Balenciaga-Givenchy-Venet*, a collection of forty sublime evening dresses selected by Hubert and Philippe themselves. The *Inoubliables Robes de mariées* (Unforgettable Wedding Dresses) exhibition was in 2012 and consisted of twenty-seven wedding dresses all lent by friends who wore the famous designers Yves Saint Laurent, Christian Dior, Christian Lacroix, Balmain, Oscar de la Renta, Jacques Fath, and Balenciaga… as well as my lovely wedding dress created by Philippe in 1978.

For ten years, from 2007, Victoria, Sebastian, and I were fortunate enough to bring the festival *Opéra en Plein Air* to Haroué to allow guests to dream under the stars while listening to the sounds of *Carmen*, *Madame Butterfly*, *La Bohème*, *La Traviata*, and *The Tales of Hoffmann*… and taking in the beauty of the nightfall descending on the castle. It was a humbling satisfaction to know that during these two evenings my family and I were surrounded by three thousand guests, some of whom were discovering opera for the first time and traveled from afar.

A couple of the challenges that I am proud to have achieved are completing the first floor as well as keeping the history of this eighteenth-century monument alive and bringing it into the twenty-first century. Thirty-nine years later, I am still awestruck by Haroué's beauty, purity, and grandeur. I am very touched by Victoria and Sebastian's love and dedication to our family home and happy to see that—thanks to my granddaughter, Isabella—the long unbroken chain is kept alive.

It is part of this wonderful journey that I wish to share as you leaf through these pages. Thanks to Victoria's unique touch, in close collaboration with her friend Peter Copping, and through the lens of Miguel's ever-perceptive eye and sensitivity, this book came to be.

FAMILY TREE

Marc de Beauvau, Prince of Craon (1679–1754)
∞ Anne-Marguerite de Ligniville († 1772)
Twenty children including

Marie-Françoise Catherine
(1711–1786)
∞ Louis-François
de Boufflers, Marquis
(1714–1751)
|
Stanislas de Boufflers,
Chevalier (1738–1815)

Charles-Just, Marshal (1720–1793)
∞ Charlotte de La Tour
d'Auvergne
(1729–1763)
|
Anne (1750–1834)
∞ Louise de Noailles,
Prince of Poix (1752–1819)

∞ Marie de
Rohan-Chabot
(1729–1807)

Ferdinand-Jérôme (1723–1790)
∞ Louise Desmiers d'Archiac (1747)

Marc-Étienne de Beauvau-Craon (1773–1849)
∞ Nathalie de Montemart (1774–1854)

Charles-Just-François-Victurnien (1793–1864)
∞ Lucie de Choiseul
Praslin (1794–1834)
|
Marc (1816–1883)
∞ Marie d'Aubusson de
La Feuillade (1824–1862)

∞ Ludmilla de Komar
(1819–1881)

Edmond (1795–1861)
∞ Valentine Du Cayla
(1806–1885)

∞ Adèle de Gontaut Biron
(1848–1938)

Henriette (1876–1931)
∞ Charles d'Harcourt (1870–1956)

Charles-Louis (1878–1942)
∞ Minnie Gregorini-Bingham (1896–1970)

Marc, seventh Prince of Beauvau-Craon (1921–1982)
∞ Cristina Patiño y Borbón (1932)   ∞ Laure Du Temple de Rougemont
(1943–2017)

Minnie de Beauvau-Craon (1953)
∞ Duncan McLaren (1944); ∞ Javier Botana (1949)

Diane de Beauvau-Craon (1955)

Victoria Botana
de Beauvau-Craon (1986)

Sebastian Botana de Beauvau-Craon (1987)
∞ Lavinia Palacios (1989)

Yunes de Beauvau-Craon
(1980)

Isabella Botana de Beauvau-Craon
(2020)

ARCHITECTURE
AND GARDENS

28

A CHÂTEAU IN HARMONY
WITH ITS NATURAL SETTING

A CHÂTEAU IN HARMONY
WITH ITS NATURAL SETTING

Back in the eighteenth century, Prince Marc de Beauvau-Craon wanted a large house, because he dreamed of having a large family. His dreams were to come true: he had Haroué built, and fathered twenty children.

Born on April 2, 1676, in Vienna, Marc de Beauvau-Craon, who then had the title of Marquis, arrived in Lorraine with his childhood friend Leopold, Duke of Lorraine, at a time when the region was recovering from the ravages of the Thirty Years' War (1618–1648). The Duke set about promulgating ordinances to re-establish his rule and revive the region's economy, which led Lorraine into a period of artistic and intellectual brilliance that came to be called its "golden age."

Duke Leopold, an extravagant character, gave his childhood friend Marc de Beauvau-Craon the title of Marquis of Haroué, with land south of Nancy, and thirty-eight surrounding communes. During the ceremony that marked his taking ownership of his new domain, Marc de Beauvau-Craon was symbolically presented with a clod of Haroué's soil.

The Marquis, who in 1725 became a Prince of the Holy Roman Empire, was also a Grandee of Spain, Grand Constable of Lorraine, Knight of the Order of the Golden Fleece, Viceroy of the Grand Duchy of Tuscany, and Governor to François III of Lorraine, Duke Leopold's son. Duke Leopold had total confidence in the Prince, and so appointed him in 1736 to negotiate François's marriage to Maria Theresa, Archduchess of Austria; the process of Lorraine's annexation by the Kingdom of France began during these negotiations.

In 1739, King Louis XV recognized the Beauvau-Craon family as "the King's cousins," in honor of Isabeau de Beauvau—daughter of Louis de Beauvau, who was the first person to translate Boccaccio into French—as her marriage to Jean VIII de Bourbon made her King Henry IV's great-great-grandmother.

In 1720, Marc de Beauvau-Craon took the decision—supported by his wife, Anne-Marguerite de Ligniville, who was a member of one of the Lorraine nobility's oldest families—to begin construction of what would be an extremely elegant château. The work went on for just over a decade. He was so impatient to live there that he moved in before it was completed, living with his family in the midst of the construction workers.

His choice of designer was the great architect Germain Boffrand (1667–1754), who had already built the Château de Lunéville for Duke Leopold—referred to as "the little Versailles of Lorraine," as well as the Hôtel de Soubise in Paris, now the National Archives—and had drawn plans for the Place de la Concorde. Boffrand was a pupil of Jules Hardouin-Mansart, who took part in the construction of Versailles. He was also First Architect to the Duke of Lorraine.

It was on the vestiges of the medieval castle of François de Bassompierre, Marshal of France, a twelfth-century fortress, that Boffrand would build the finest château in Lorraine. The château is at the bottom of a valley, right by the water: beside it lies the Madon, a little river that runs calmly and gently through the peaceful Saintois countryside. Looming up in the middle of this landscape planted with mirabelle orchards, wheat, sunflower and rapeseed fields, and deep forests, the Beauvau-Craon family's castle is dazzling. So refined, so elegant, so imposing…

"It is not enough for a building to be handsome; it must be pleasing, and the onlooker must sense the character that it is intended to convey—in such a way that it must appear cheerful to those to whom it is meant to communicate joy, and serious and melancholy to those in whom it is meant to instill respect or sadness." (G. Boffrand, *Book of Architecture*)

Boffrand was an architect and an interior designer, and one of the key players in the French Regency style, which he helped to create. Keen to preserve classical monumentality while also asserting a sort of architectural modernity, he reserved the exuberance of rocaille decoration for the interiors.

"A banqueting hall or ballroom must not be made like a church. By the same principle, a private individual's house must not be planned and decorated like a sovereign's palace, or a prince's palace like a church. In each one of these modes or orders of architecture, the significant characteristics most suited to each building can be found." (G. Boffrand, *Book of Architecture*)

For his wealthy private clientele, he applied the aristocratic codes of his time: reception rooms at ground level, "noble" apartments on the first floor. He theorized his practice in his *Book of Architecture*, published in 1745, which contains the general principles of the art, and what was considered "good taste." In it, he describes the Château de Haroué in detail.

In his words: "The château belonging to the Prince of Craon stands in Lorraine, pleasantly sited by the Madon river. It consists of a forecourt that is separated from the main body of the château by a wide moat of living water that encircles the main building and the wings flanked by four towers. Alongside the château, there is a large service yard where the stables, carriage sheds, and other amenities of a large house can be found."

He continues: "The plan of the main building comprises two apartments; the wing to the right, a chapel and two apartments; the wing to the left, the kitchens and pantries. The floor above contains two large apartments and other smaller ones. The top floor is also devoted to several apartments as well as lodgings for the serving staff."

Concerned to "preserve the soundness of the beautiful proportions," he designed the facades for the main building overlooking the courtyard and garden, ornamenting them with a peristyle composed of Ionic columns offering a covered entrance to the ground floor, with a Corinthian order on the first floor.

With four round towers topped by pepper-pot roofs, as well as twelve turrets, fifty-two chimneys, 365 windows, and eighty-two rooms, Haroué is an allegory of passing time. The greatest artists of Lorraine contributed to its embellishment. Jean Lamour (1698–1771), designer of the gilded railings on the Place Stanislas in Nancy, was responsible for those of the château's main courtyard, grand staircase, and balconies. They display the interwoven "C"s of the Craon family that can also be seen on the balconies of the Hôtel de Craon, Marc de Beauvau-Craon's residence in Nancy, which serves today as the Court of Appeal.

Reflected in the water of the moat, to the front and rear of the château, are groups of cherub statues that serve as reminders of Marc de Beauvau-Craon's taste for the fine arts, painting, music, gardening… Those on the garden side bear the family's coat of arms and the Constable's sword. They are the work of Barthélemy Guibal (1699–1757), appointed First Sculptor to Duke Leopold in 1724.

As for the chapel, located at ground level in the west wing, its altar and paneling are attributed to César Bagard. The remains of the last Prince of Beauvau-Craon were laid to rest in this chapel in

1982, and the chapel is still used today to celebrate family events. Sebastian and Lavinia were married here on May 28, 2018, and their daughter, Isabella, was christened here.

Alongside Germain Boffrand's château stand outbuildings that date from the seventeenth century, which today are called the "Château Bassompierre." Two dovecotes remain from this medieval ensemble, with their pigeonholes intact. The number of these indicated the owner's wealth. Still intact, and resembling a secure defensive system, the Bassompierre gate acts as an entrance to the service areas, all roofed in terracotta fishscale tile. Also found here are the stables, as well as a very fine tack room that still contains all of the Beauvau-Craon lords' high-quality harnesses, saddles, and other horse-riding equipment from across the centuries. As a reminder of this bygone era, Minnie allows Winnie and Dahlia—two chestnut-colored Pottok ponies given to her by her cousin Albina du Boisrouvray—to roam about among the orchard's mirabelle and cherry trees.

A hedge of clipped hornbeams has been planted to separate the slightly wild orchard from the garden created by Minnie Gregorini-Bingham, the current Princess's Italian grandmother, who called upon her English friend Russell Page to design it. The so-called "English garden" is 70 meters (230 feet) long and extends the full length of the Château

Bassompierre. It is ornamented with box trees clipped into cone shapes, and stone statues representing baskets of vegetables, a gift from the Duke of Talleyrand to Marc de Beauvau-Craon in 1960. Minnie added her own personal touch upon the birth of her daughter, Victoria, by planting tree peonies and rose trees in white and blue tones. Box topiary in the form of swans, planted in 2000, represents the Princess and her two children and the coming into the new century.

The Château de Haroué is also in harmony with its natural environment. On his return in 1945 from the war—during which he had joined General Charles de Gaulle in London at a very early stage, in 1941—Prince Marc de Beauvau-Craon took charge again of the château's destiny, but the grounds were not his first priority. After years of neglect, they had in reality become… a field!

To create the garden, the Prince approached his friend Emilio Terry, the Cuban architect and designer of interiors and landscapes, in 1957. Under Terry's direction, a French-style garden sprung up with the château as its focal point, alongside the grove of trees that itself dates from the eighteenth century. Eight alleys radiate in a star formation from the central water feature, passing between chestnut trees that are several hundred years old. Terry devised a highly classical park setting for Haroué, the originality of which resides in the fact that it opens out onto a view over the countryside of Lorraine, thus earning its name of "palace in the fields" more than ever. In July 1957, Terry provided a first design, a watercolor titled "Design for the green carpet, Château de Haroué." He notably visualized box hedging in a Greek key pattern, ornamented in several places with the crowned letter B for Beauvau, and envisaged extending the inlet from the Madon river. But he gave up on this idea with the owner's agreement, Marc de Beauvau-Craon preferring a simpler garden. Terry's "green carpet" extends from the river to the grove of trees.

The harmony of the French-style park, guarded at the far end by two enigmatic stone sphinxes, stems from its stripped-back, very simple look. It is planted with hornbeams that are trimmed alternately into a conical or a trapezoid shape. Beyond, the gentle countryside of Lorraine unfolds, just as Claude Gellée—better known as Claude Lorrain—might have painted it. The qualities of the Lorraine countryside are perfectly illustrated here. "It is neither spectacular nor picturesque," wrote Françoise Hervé, then a site inspector, "but the great beauty of the landscape that stretches out from the park into the countryside inspires a sense of peace. This is what justified the park and landscape being granted protected status by the State in July 1990. It is a measure that covers 882 hectares [2,179 acres] and the surrounding villages."

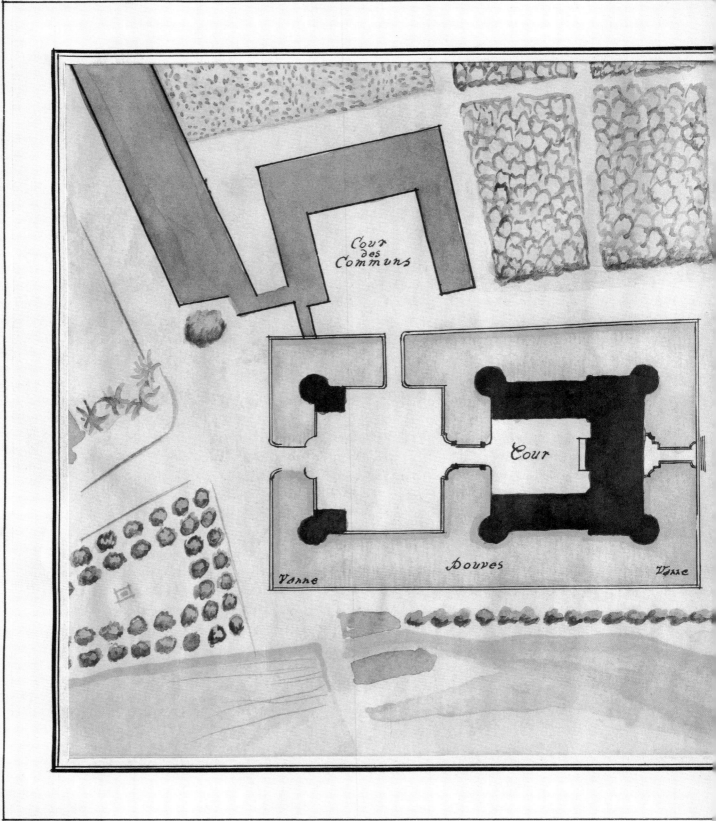

Cour
des
Communs

Cour

Vanne   Douves   Vanne

Château

Avant projet

par

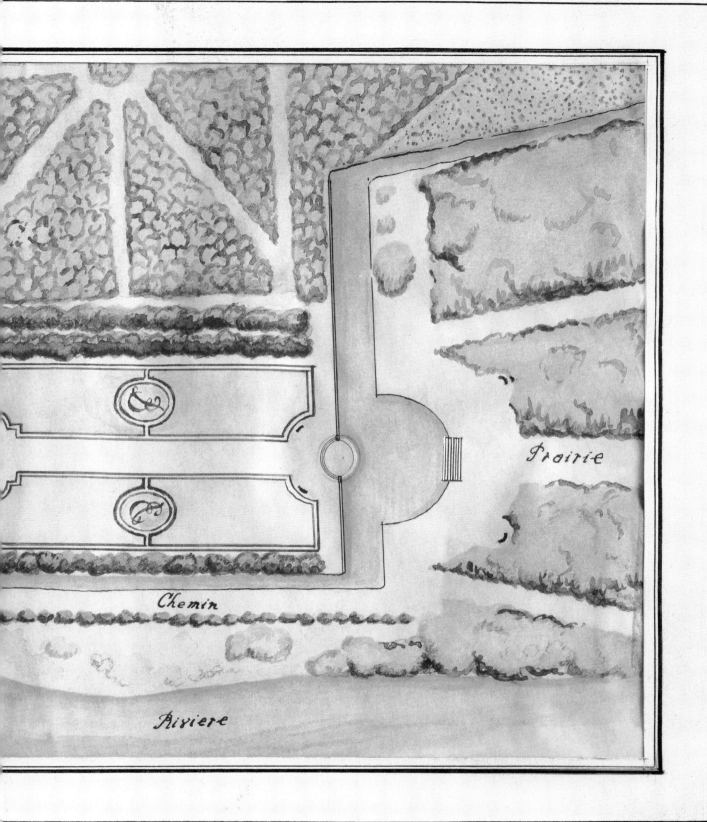

Prairie

Chemin

Riviere

'aroué

e Tapis Vert

Terry

"Haroué has been here for centuries and is part of history, our family's history of course, but also that of all who have passed through its gates and who in one way or another have left their mark.

Haroué is part of my DNA and forms a big part of my identity. It helped shape me into the woman I am today. I love to open my house to friends for a weekend or for a special celebration and I love the energy that each guest brings to it. This flow of people is what allows it to remain of its time. This house is not only our past but also our future, and it is most important for me to share its history and the energy it gives me with others.

Each generation has worked hard to perpetuate its beauty, and each and every one of us has brought their own imprint to the house. This place is a multi-generational labor of love; our passion for this place has allowed it to stay alive and up to date. Some monuments have a soul and can move you. Haroué is one of them.

Not a day goes by where Haroué is not on my mind, and every time I come I am always amazed by its beauty and its lasting power. Each one of its stones brings me strength, and the gardens and fields surrounding it have been throughout my life the starting point of my most beautiful dreams."

—VICTORIA BOTANA DE BEAUVAU-CRAON

THE CELLARS

74

THE FOUNDATIONS OF THE CHÂTEAU

THE FOUNDATIONS OF THE CHÂTEAU

"The cellars are vaulted throughout; those beneath the main building are used as an orangery, and those between the wings as summer rooms and other amenities for the house," wrote Germain Boffrand in his 1745 *Book of Architecture*.

It is here, within this stone-built space bathed in golden light, where the water in the moat casts shimmering reflections, that one becomes aware of the château's density and fragility. The moat is the oldest part of the castle.

In 2000, Minnie de Beauvau-Craon wanted to bring contemporary art into her eighteenth-century château. With Victoria, Sebastian, and artist friends, the orangery was transformed into an exhibition space painted in limewash throughout the 600 square meters (6,500 square feet); the reflection of the moat on the space brought an extraordinary quality of light to the cellars.

In 2003, the artist Leonora Hamill inaugurated "The Space" with a photographic exhibition on Cambodia, followed by Marie Hugo's paintings; then came Gérald Incandela with his unique photographs and the painter Wilfried Prager, followed by the Argentine painter Alberto Bali, whose delicate watercolors depicting the château over the four seasons were the illustrations of a very personal book *La Consolation de Haroué*, written by Daniel Rondeau, a friend of the family and member of the Académie Française, the official authority on the French language.

In 2009, in the run-up to the opening of the Centre Pompidou-Metz, its curator, Laurent Le Bon, chose to hold one of its photographic exhibitions—*Constellations*—off-site at Haroué. The château thus became one of the stopping-off points in a trail dedicated to contemporary art in Lorraine.

The painter Beatrice Caracciolo took over the entire orangery in 2012, presenting a specially conceived exhibition, "… *pour que passe enfin mon torrent d'anges*" ("… for my flight of angels to come at last"), which filled the space and lent it an unsuspected dimension. The gray or oxidized zinc that she cut, manipulated, stretched, and distorted married well with the bare stones of the château's foundations. The path she traced through the immaculate whiteness of the heavily vaulted cellars was enlivened by reflections from the moat, and provided space for daydreaming. Or for angels…

THE STATE ROOMS

HISTORY IN ALL ITS GLORY

As soon as you arrive at the château, you are immersed in an eighteenth-century atmosphere, which its current owners are keen to preserve. Once you have crossed the vast gravel courtyard, you must ascend five stone steps watched over by an imposing colonnade, before entering the vestibule. This main entrance is elegant in its simplicity and grandeur. From here, you can access the *salle d'armes*, which offers a sweeping perspectival view over the gardens beyond.

In the eighteenth century, this large room served as an antechamber, a dining room, and a billiard room. Billiards was all the rage in the court at Lunéville, and Prince Marc de Beauvau-Craon, who built Haroué, enthusiastically joined the frenzy. He lost a great deal of money at it, but his debts were compensated by Duke Leopold's largesse.

Today, the family's swords are evocative of the Beauvau-Craons' past glories on the battlefield. Two richly crafted sabers, gifts from King Mohammed V of Morocco to Princess Minnie's grandfather, recall the sharifian monarch's friendship with Marshal Lyautey, whom he visited in his Lorraine residence of Thorey-Lyautey, 9 kilometers (6 miles) away.

To the right, Princess Anne-Marguerite de Ligniville's apartments recount tales from the Lorraine region's history. They are comprised of a grand enfilade leading to the Salon Pillement, in the west tower. A first salon with large-scale tapestries depicts the epic story of Alexander the Great. It was in this "large study" that Anne-Marguerite de Ligniville would receive distinguished guests. The decor, designed by Boffrand, is feminine. Above the marble fireplace, musical instruments and garlands of flowers bring a softness to the otherwise formal room. Then, the state chamber is a room that has seen history being made—for it was here, on March 12, 1737, that the Council of Independent Lorraine met for the last time, presided over by Duke Leopold's widow, Élisabeth-Charlotte d'Orléans (1676–1744). At the end of the enfilade is the Salon Pillement, a circular room that is exquisite in its freshness and originality, decorated with Chinese motifs. Here, the architect Germain Boffrand managed to gracefully exploit the medieval heritage by designing little circular studies in round towers at the château's east and west extremities, each with four windows, with balconies offering views of the park.

Boffrand opted to place the main staircase in the château's east wing, in order to preserve the beautiful proportions of the ground-floor reception rooms. This staircase, with a wrought-iron balustrade by Jean Lamour, offers the opportunity to admire the owners' family tree, hand-painted on parchment in 1722 by the heraldry specialist at that time, François Chevillard. On the upper part, an inscription painted in red reads: "Family tree of the House of Beauvau, descended from the former Counts of Anjou." The grand staircase is adorned on both sides by large portraits of the family members who commissioned the building of the château. Further on, as you arrive at the next level, you see engravings of the cartoons by Charles Le Brun that served as models for the ground-floor tapestries, displayed in the *salle d'armes* and the two adjacent rooms.

LA VERTV EST DIGNE DE L'EMPIRE DV MONDE.

DIGNA ORBIS IMPERIO VIRTVS

THE ENTRANCE

The peristyle's black-and-white checkerboard floor is worn, polished by three centuries of visitors. Gazing down upon two richly decorated, gilded wood sedan chairs are two family portraits, of Jean and Louis de Beauvau, two brothers who were equerries to King Henry IV (1553–1610), whose great-great-grandmother was Isabeau de Beauvau, Jean de Bourbon's wife. One of the chairs, in crimson silk velvet that has over the centuries lost its sheen, once belonged to Anne-Marguerite de Ligniville, Marc de Beauvau-Craon's wife; it appears as if she had just gotten out of it to make her way to the grand salon where her guests await her.

The second one has a more eventful history. Minnie acquired it at auction in Saint-Dié, in the Vosges region. "I'd seen this wonderful sedan chair, which I found all the more interesting because it featured the Beauvau-Craon coat of arms and was decorated with the Constable's sword," the Princess recalls. "It had been converted into a bar and needed a lot of restoration work! I hoped I could make the purchase discreetly, because the sellers hadn't noticed I was there and hadn't spotted the family crest. But it didn't last. Someone recognized me, and the price went up." Minnie finally acquired the sedan chair. Its blue, gold, and russet-colored studded Cordoba leather roof-covering needed to have its sheen reinstated, and the interior to be entirely reupholstered.

Then followed an unexpected discovery. "While the chair was being restored, the craftsman contacted me. He had just found a stash of bills, 30,000 francs at the time, underneath the floor of the chair, and was planning to give the whole lot to me. It was so loyal and honest that I gave him half. Since he was about to have a child, the sum went toward the baby's nursery."

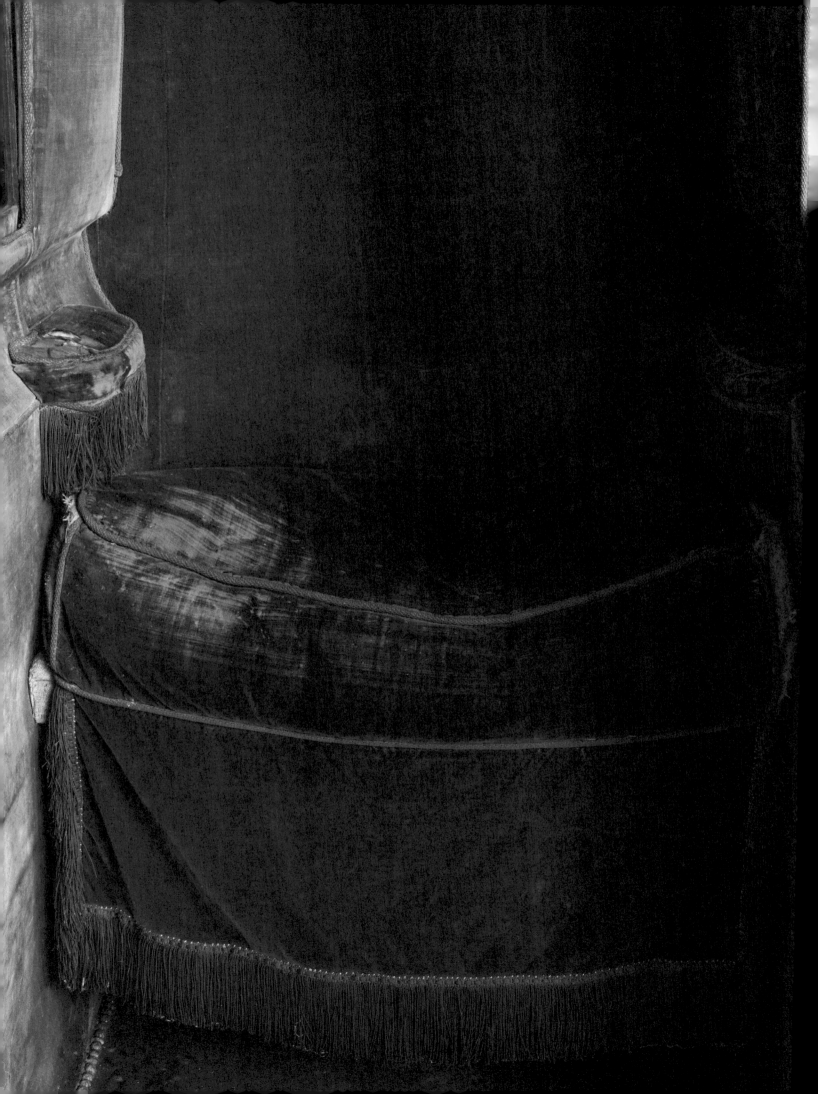

THE WOVEN STORY OF ALEXANDER THE GREAT:
ELEVEN STATELY TAPESTRIES

Open to the public, the ground floor is devoted to the eighteenth century. Here you can admire a collection of eleven exceptional tapestries that depict Alexander the Great's battles against Darius, King of Persia, after cartoons by Charles Le Brun (1619–1690), who was King Louis XIV's official painter as well as director of the Gobelins Manufactory royal tapestry workshops.

From the seventeenth to the eighteenth century, tapestry was considered a high art, and the Lorraine region took pride in being home to several workshops where very talented loom setters from Paris, who had often trained at the Gobelins or in Flanders, created masterpieces. It took years to produce these large-format tapestries that portrayed scenes from mythology or the region's history. It is believed to have taken each weaver a whole year to create one square meter (or yard) of tapestry. These flamboyant pieces came from the La Malgrange ducal workshop, on the outskirts of Nancy. They were Duke Leopold's gift to his friend Marc de Beauvau-Craon for his marriage in 1704 at Lunéville. The beautiful borders are surmounted

by the crests of Marc de Beauvau-Craon and Anne-Marguerite de Ligniville, side by side. The Duke himself had received permission from the King of France, Louis XIV, to reproduce them.

The large tapestry that covers the entire wall of the room next to the *salle d'armes* depicts Darius's women coming to make offerings at Alexander the Great's feet. Alexander is standing, while the women bow down; he wears a plumed helmet, and is accompanied by Hephaestion, his companion-in-arms, whom he loved with a brotherly passion. Highly expressive and particularly opulent, these tapestries are a perfect example of know-how in Lorraine in the eighteenth century, and they testify to the family's power and wealth.

Following Prince Marc de Beauvau-Craon's death in 1982, his daughters, Minnie and Diane, donated these tapestries—which have been accorded national historic monument status—to the French state, in lieu of death duties. An agreement was reached between the owner and the state, so that the tapestries could remain in trust at the Château de Haroué.

A STATELY ROOM THAT MADE HISTORY

This ground-floor room at Haroué, lined with red silk damask and home to an imposing seventeenth-century Italian canopy bed bearing the "Ave Maria" monogram, was the site of a key moment in the history of both the Lorraine region and France as a whole. Anne-Marguerite de Ligniville's state bedchamber was the setting for the signature of the first legal papers related to France's annexation of Lorraine. It was here that the heartbroken Duchess of Lorraine, Leopold's widow, signed the documents that ratified Lorraine's loss of independence. Before going into exile, the Duchess of Lorraine had spent a week resting at Haroué.

In 1737, Stanisław Leszczyński—the fallen King of Poland—was given Lorraine to govern for his lifetime, acquiring the title of Duke of Lorraine and of Bar. He came to stay at Haroué for a while, before taking possession of his château at Lunéville. He was the successor to Leopold, who had died in 1729. The Duke Stanisław's daughter Marie Leszczyńska became Queen of France through her marriage to Louis XV. The King of France thought that this interim reign would be brief. In fact, it lasted twenty-nine years.

It was agreed that, after Stanisław's death in 1766, the much-coveted region of Lorraine would come under French rule. Antoine-Martin Chaumont de la Galaizière would oversee the process. He was appointed to the task by the King of France. In the meantime, Lorraine experienced its golden age. During his reign, Stanisław—a philosophical, debonair ruler who loved science, good food, gardens, and festivities—won his subjects' hearts. His maxim was always: "True happiness consists in making people happy."

The memory of this historic moment remains in the state bedchamber. A little red chalk drawing of King Stanisław, given to Princess Minnie de Beauvau-Craon by Liliane de Rothschild, and a portrait of the sovereign painted in oil on canvas, recall how close the Beauvau-Craon family were to the court of Lorraine—historically they played a key role in it. Indeed, Marc de Beauvau-Craon's wife, the beautiful Anne-Marguerite de Ligniville, was the love of Duke Leopold's life. For him, the last sovereign Duke of Lorraine, it was love at first sight, and he was very generous to both her and her husband—his childhood friend—with gifts and honors. The Duke nevertheless remained very fond of his spouse, Élisabeth-Charlotte d'Orléans… It was a situation that King Louis XIV is said to have found very entertaining: he would have details of the scandalous affairs of the court of Lorraine recounted to him by the Princess Palatine, Élizabeth-Charlotte's mother, wife of Philippe d'Orléans, the King's brother.

M. le Chevalier de Boufflers

POSTERITÉ D'ISABEAU
BEAUVAU EPOUSE DE IEAN
OURBON COMTE DE VENDOSME
DEDIEÉ
Haut et Tres Puissant Seigneur
uc Marquis de Beauvau de Craon Grand
Ecuier de Lorraine
ur.

honneur qu'un Gentilhomme de bonne Maison puisse avoir, c'est
igine. jl y en a cependant qui lignorent et jl leur est quelquefois avantageux

SALON PILLEMENT
AND THE IRRESISTIBLE MARQUISE DE BOUFFLERS

If there is one charming, slightly libertine character who best illustrates the art and pleasure of eighteenth-century life at Haroué, it is Marie-Françoise-Catherine de Beauvau-Craon, later Marquise de Boufflers. She was the sixth child of Marc and Anne-Marguerite de Ligniville, who had twenty in all. It is amusing to imagine them all in the chinoiserie-decorated salon in the Pillement tower. At the time, it was a music room lit by candles, whose reflections rebounded around the mirrors with their gilded wooden frames. The exquisite oriental wall decors are by Jean Pillement (1728–1808), a painter who was very fashionable in the eighteenth century and admired by Queen Marie Antoinette. His elegant Chinese subjects illustrate the taste of the period for the East and its exoticism. Amid a landscape of pagodas are small figures carrying silk paper parasols, birds taking flight, fantastical beasts, and arabesques on a very soft gray-blue ground with gold accents. This delightful room is one of the last expressions in France of such decors featuring chinoiserie motifs. Two other examples are known: the Singeries at the Château de Chantilly, and the boudoir and Salon Chinois at the Château de Champs-sur-Marne. The salon served as a showcase for Marie-Françoise-Catherine, who decorated it with pieces of Chinese porcelain. This very unique tower was restored in 1984, thanks to the generosity of American Friends of French Art.

Marie-Françoise-Catherine was intelligent, loved art, sought out the company of philosophers, counted Voltaire and Montesquieu among her visitors, and displayed her wit in the customary eighteenth-century manner. She "loved partying and being happy," and had several lovers at the same time... including Stanisław, the last King of Poland and Duke of Lorraine. She was well-read and had a way with words. She wrote her epitaph herself, and it completely sums her up:

> Ci-gît dans une paix profonde
> Cette dame de volupté
> Qui, pour plus de sûreté,
> Fit son paradis dans ce monde.
> (Here lies, in deep peace,
> This lady of delight
> Who, just to be sure,
> Made her paradise in this world.)

A portrait of Marie-Françoise-Catherine as a child hangs in the salon-library, and shows a gorgeous young girl in a blue-and-silver silk dress covered with roses. To imagine how she looked as an adult, we have to refer to a description of her by her son Stanislas de Boufflers: "Even in her prime, her face was never strictly speaking beautiful or pretty, but she was to the prettiest what the prettiest sometimes are to the most beautiful. She was more attractive." She clearly possessed what might be called "charm." Her pale complexion, fine waist, and dazzling smile, together with the way she moved, combining an air of nobility with a wildness of spirit, made her irresistible. She loved reading, and was very talented at both drawing and writing.

She enjoyed play-acting with Voltaire and his beloved companion, Madame du Châtelet, with whom she was quite happy to share the handsome poet and military officer Saint-Lambert without the slightest drama.

She was educated until the age of twenty-three in Remiremont Abbey in the Vosges region—a very secular convent of canonesses, entrants to which were required to be of noble descent right up to the level of all their great-great-grandparents. She learned good manners there, but the nuns' diligent efforts had little influence on her moral principles. A year after leaving the convent, she married Marquis Louis-François de Boufflers… but he preferred to be away waging war rather than attend to his young wife. Bored of this arrangement, Marie-Françoise-Catherine returned to live with her mother, Duke Leopold's muse. To combat her boredom, she cheated on her husband. She is known to have had a relationship with a certain François-Antoine Devaux, from Lunéville, whom his friends called Panpan. An amiable poet and revenue collector at Lunéville, he was good-looking and witty, and was a much-loved companion to Marie-Françoise-Catherine for the rest of her life.

On the arrival of King Stanisław, successor to Duke Leopold, she met Antoine-Martin Chaumont de la Galaizière, whom Louis XV had appointed Chancellor of Lorraine. La Galaizière was a powerful man who very few could resist. But, faced with the lovely Marquise, he is the one who surrendered—she was one of the most witty women at Stanisław's court at the Château de Lunéville. As for the former King of Poland, he too would often visit her in her palace at Haroué. Festivities held there sparkled during long and mellow evenings. There would be card-playing until dawn, conversation, philosophizing, dancing, play-acting, harp-playing…

At Haroué, the atmosphere was as light as a champagne bubble. And Stanisław the Benefactor himself found the spirited, joyous Marquise enticing. She is the one who wrote:

De plaire un jour sans aimer j'eus l'envie ;
Je ne cherchais qu'un simple amusement.
L'amusement devint un sentiment ;
Le sentiment, le bonheur de ma vie…
(I fancied a brief flirtation—not love;
I was seeking no more than amusement.
The amusement then became sentiment;
And that sentiment, my life's greatest bliss…)

But despite the Polish King's boredom with his wife, who was often depressed, he was also "encumbered" with a mistress, Duchess Ossolińska, who had followed him from Poland. When she died in 1756, followed by Catherine, his Queen, the coast was clear…

Stanisław was then seventy years old; Marie-Françoise-Catherine, forty-five. La Galaizière proved to be understanding. She became Stanisław's mistress, his "lady of delight," while she kept a tender relationship with La Galaizière.

The delightful Marquise de Boufflers remained by Stanisław's side until the very end. Legend even has it that his final witty gibe was addressed to her as he died in her arms. Badly burned from a fall near his fireplace, Stanisław was in pain. As she cradled him, he spoke his last words:

"Madame, must I still burn so fiercely for you, at my age?"

The Marquise died in 1786, aged seventy-four, and did not witness her daughter, Marquise de Boisgelin, being beheaded during the French Revolution.

THE ROYAL APARTMENT

GILDED GOLD ROOM: SALON HÉBERT

The Salon Hébert, a continuation of the enfilade of Louis XVIII rooms, is a symphony in gold and gray with its decorative scheme inspired by antiquity. Here again, there is a story behind this sumptuous decor... Charles-Just, fourth Prince of Beauvau-Craon, who was an enthusiastic art collector, undertook the restoration and redecoration of this room in 1858, along with his wife, Ludmilla.

The work was intended to offer a sumptuous welcome to Emperor Napoleon III (1808–1873), who had announced that he would be visiting Haroué. He regularly went to take the waters at Plombières, and since Haroué was on the way... To give the room real éclat, Prince Charles-Just, a Senator of the Second Empire, commissioned the painter Ernest Hébert (1817–1908), who was Director of the Medici Villa and had won the Rome Prize in 1839. His inspiration for Haroué was the Cabinet des Muses at the Hôtel Lambert in Paris, painted by the great seventeenth-century artist Eustache le Sueur.

The wood paneling is gilded in gold leaf, and four large caryatids decorate the panels to either side of the oxblood-colored Aleppo marble fireplace. The symbolism in vogue in the nineteenth century is illustrated by representations of the signs of the zodiac and allegories that feature on the door panels. Putti flit about on the ceiling. Small figures painted on the door panels recount the months of the year, and the overdoors illustrate the seasons.

For his models, the painter—who came to work at Haroué several times—used four attractive young women of Polish aristocratic origin: three sisters from the Komar family and their cousin Honorine. One of the Komar sisters was Ludmilla, who would become Princess of Beauvau-Craon. Her siblings Nathalie, Princess Medici-Spada, and Delphine, Countess Potocka, together with their cousin Honorine Possiamoska, could not have been lovelier subjects. The three beautiful sisters loved the arts and practiced them with talent; they must have set many hearts aflutter, starting with Frédéric Chopin, who came to visit the Prince of Beauvau-Craon at Haroué several times. Indeed, Delphine was his student and muse, and the master of Romantic music dedicated a very pretty, cheerful waltz to her, titled *Minute Waltz* or *Waltz of the Puppy*, a piece for piano in D-flat major—Op. 64, No. 1.

But the cheerful echoes of this waltz can do nothing to erase the memory of a dramatic event that occurred in this room and marked the end of Haroué's heyday for many years. One day, when he was perched at the top of a ladder to adjust the drape of a curtain, Charles-Just fell, leaving him paralyzed from the waist down. He left Haroué to live in Paris, in a hôtel particulier that is now the Ministry of the Interior—built by his ancestor Marshal Charles-Just de Beauvau-Craon, Governor of the Languedoc region, War Minister to Louis XVI, and member of the Académie Française—where he steadfastly continued to take care of his region's affairs. He died there, exhausted, in 1864, without ever having returned to Haroué. His wife, Ludmilla, would never return there either…

Haroué's subsequent fate saw several twists and turns, some more romantic than others. Marc de Beauvau-Craon, Charles's son, decided to get rid of the artworks and to sell the château itself. The memory of his father's accident had made him despise the house.

Meanwhile, the brothers Prosper and Jules Tourtel, successful brewers based in nearby Tantonville, coveted the vast volumes of the cellars, for their ideal humidity levels. They dreamed of using them as a storage area to dry hops. They bought the château, but were its owners for no more than twenty-four hours. A good fairy was watching over Haroué, narrowly sparing it an industrial destiny.

That good fairy was Princess Valentine du Cayla, wife of Edmond de Beauvau-Craon and daughter of Zoé du Cayla. She repurchased Haroué two days after the sale, for her son Marie-Joseph-Louis de Beauvau-Craon—an only child who died in 1868 aged just forty-two. Upon Valentine's death in 1884, it was her nephew Charles-Louis who inherited it, becoming head of the family at only six years old. He was the current owner's grandfather. Also included in his inheritance was the royal furniture from the Château de Saint-Ouen that Louis XVIII had given to Zoé, Countess du Cayla.

In 1884, like Sleeping Beauty, Haroué fell into a deep slumber that would last forty years…

In 1914, Maurice Barrès, a writer and politician from Lorraine, urged Prince Charles-Louis de Beauvau-Craon to come back to Haroué. "It is to that place," he wrote, "on that vast lonely plain of Sion, where the finest château awaits him fully intact, that I dearly wish to bring the young prince, so that he might reawaken his domain and worthily take part in the renaissance of our province, as he desires to do."

A young Italian beauty—another good fairy— would breathe new life into this château that decidedly owes a great deal to women. Bologna-born Minnie Gregorini-Bingham, Charles-Louis de Beauvau-Craon's fiancée, fell in love with Haroué. The aristocratic couple, who married in 1920, were familiar faces on Paris's social scene and dazzled at the wildest costume balls, yet they chose a more bucolic setting to live in. Minnie preferred the gentle harmony of this palace-in-the-fields to the hustle and bustle of Paris. They only had one son, Marc, born on February 3, 1921. He was the seventh and last Prince of Beauvau-Craon. Minnie managed to persuade Charles-Louis to move to Haroué. In order to restore it, together they decided to sell the Château de Sainte-Assise, on the banks of the River Seine near Paris, which had been in the family's possession since 1827, along with its 3,000 hectares (7,000 acres) of land. It was a formidable task: every aspect of Haroué needed work. "My grandmother adored Haroué," recalls Princess Minnie. "She's the one who brought the Italian influence here, the cheerful pastel colors." She is buried in the family vault, in the village cemetery.

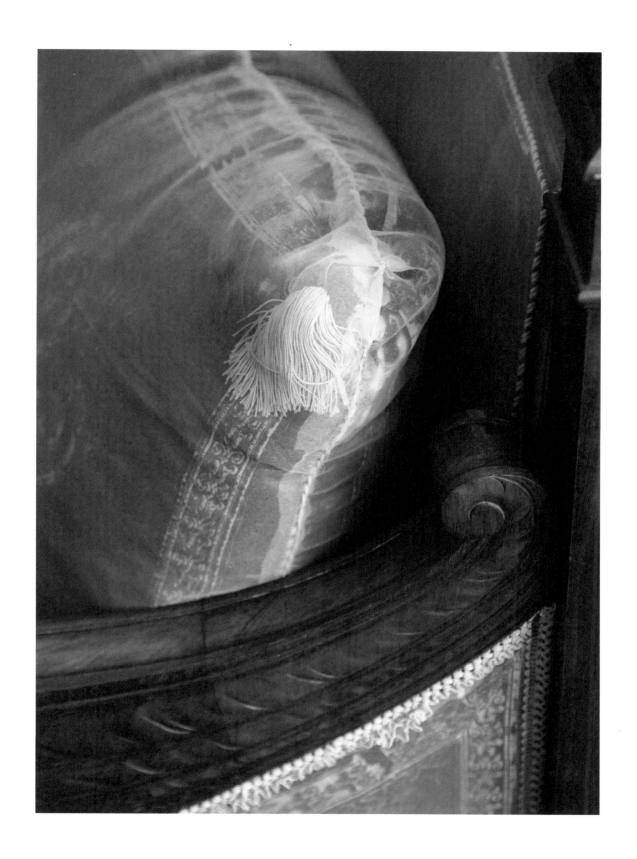

THE KING'S FURNITURE (LOUIS XVIII, 1755–1824) IN PRIVATE HANDS

During the Second Empire, Prince Charles-Just-François-Victurnien de Beauvau-Craon (1793–1864) planned to refurbish the upper floor containing the apartments and to create a gallery adjoining the Salon Hébert that would extend the full length of the château. He wanted to hang his collection of very valuable large paintings there: two Canalettos, *The Rialto Bridge* and *Saint Mark's Square*; a Van Dyck, *Portrait of Marie-Anne Schotten*; a Clouet, *Louise de Lorraine, Queen of France, Wife of Henry III*… Fate decided otherwise: after the Prince's fall and his consequent move away from the château, Haroué fell into a deep slumber.

In 1998, Princess Minnie took up the challenge of completing the refurbishment of the château's interiors, which had not changed since 1737. She had an impressive ally for the purpose: the École Boulle, one of the most prestigious applied arts schools. Its students were given free rein to create from scratch a new decor that had never been seen before, with the exception of a very fine set of neoclassical wood paneling. "There were no ceilings, and the floor was made of planks of bare wood," Minnie recalls. This level of the house had served as an enchanted world for Minnie and Diane. As children, they would play hide-and-seek there, or take refuge when they wanted to escape from their parents.

The work began in 1998, starting with the central salon. The students designed a scheme that was faithful to the spirit of the nineteenth century—such a rich period for the decorative arts—so as to provide a worthy setting for King Louis XVIII's furniture. Framed with Corinthian pilasters, emphasizing the salon's grandeur, mirrors were hung on the walls to make the space seem larger and reflect the light from the grounds around the room. This was where King Louis XVIII's salon furniture, bearing the maker's mark of Pierre-Antoine Bellangé, found its home. This set of royal furniture is made of gilded wood and includes, among other things, a large settee with its original upholstery of soft green silk brocade with white motifs. One can imagine Louis XVIII, Stanisław's great-grandson, sitting on this enormous settee, chatting to his niece, Madame Royale, Louis XVI's eldest daughter. On the floor is a large Aubusson carpet in aqua tones. The gilding on the furniture is heightened by the twinkling of a forty-eight-light Baccarat crystal chandelier. This sublime piece was given to the Princess by the manufacturer following an exhibition on Baccarat's crystal art in 1999.

In 2001, the École Boulle tackled the subject of what to do with the billiard room situated between the central salon and the Salon Hébert. The space had been stripped bare. The Boulle students designed classic wall paneling alternating with silk-covered panels made by the Prelle firm. The floor is an exact replica of the one in the *salle d'armes* on the ground floor. The furniture in this salon comprises a billiard table together with four impressive settees and a set of billiard chairs, upholstered in blue-and-white silk and made of solid mahogany decorated with a lion-headed griffin motif. These are lined up along the walls, as was the custom in the nineteenth century. The same griffin motif is found on the billiard table's legs. The reconstruction of this, in the spirit of the time, was the work of the École Boulle students, who offered it to the château as a gift.

The royal furniture was a gift from King Louis XVIII to his mistress, Zoé Victoire Talon, Countess du Cayla (1785–1852), who was thirty years his junior. A beautiful woman with pale skin and black hair, her cheerful character lit up the king's final years; she was his last muse. A large portrait that hangs in the billiard room shows her with her children, Ugolin, who died in a duel, and Valentine, who became Princess of Beauvau-Craon when she married Edmond. It was Valentine who brought this set of early nineteenth-century royal furniture to the Château de Haroué, transferring it from the Château de Saint-Ouen—another gift from the king to her mother—in Lorraine. The furniture has never left Haroué in the past 160 years.

Wanting to ensure coherence in the decor, Minnie had the fortunate opportunity to buy some period wallpaper at the Drouot auction house that bears the cipher of Charles X, brother of Louis XVI and Louis XVIII, together with a fleur-de-lys motif on a royal blue ground. This salon serves as an antechamber for the Louis XVIII suite.

Not to be forgotten is Madame du Cayla's bedchamber. Known as the "Louis XVIII" room, it contains the furniture that Valentine, Princess of Beauvau-Craon, had brought here upon her mother, Zoé du Cayla's, death. This includes an elegant mahogany *lit bateau* (boat bed), with carved wood and sculpted bronze decoration representing acanthus leaves and poppies. Another element is a cheval glass topped by three gilded bronze palmettes and equipped with a pair of candleholders, each consisting of two dragon-shaped arms. The room is lined with Pierre Frey fabric featuring a golden-yellow ground striped with a blue motif. Sunlight and time have slightly tempered the fabric's original brightness. A series of grisaille engravings representing the signs of the zodiac hang on the walls.

The final spaces remaining to be refurbished were four small rooms reminiscent of an attic, on the opposite side of what is now the Louis XVIII salon. Philippe Venet and Hubert de Givenchy—both regular visitors to Haroué, where they would come to spend weekends or set up exhibitions—had the idea of making them into a single large room, reflecting the proportions of the preceding spaces. The plain, wide-boarded flooring was retained and simply painted white. A breathtaking grisaille trompe-l'oeil decor was applied to the walls—a contemporary reproduction taken from plates of the scheme created by François Girardon, sculptor to King Louis XIV, for the Apollo Gallery at the Louvre. "Although it is very bold, this suggestion made it possible to complete this floor of the château in a way that is both beautiful and spectacular."

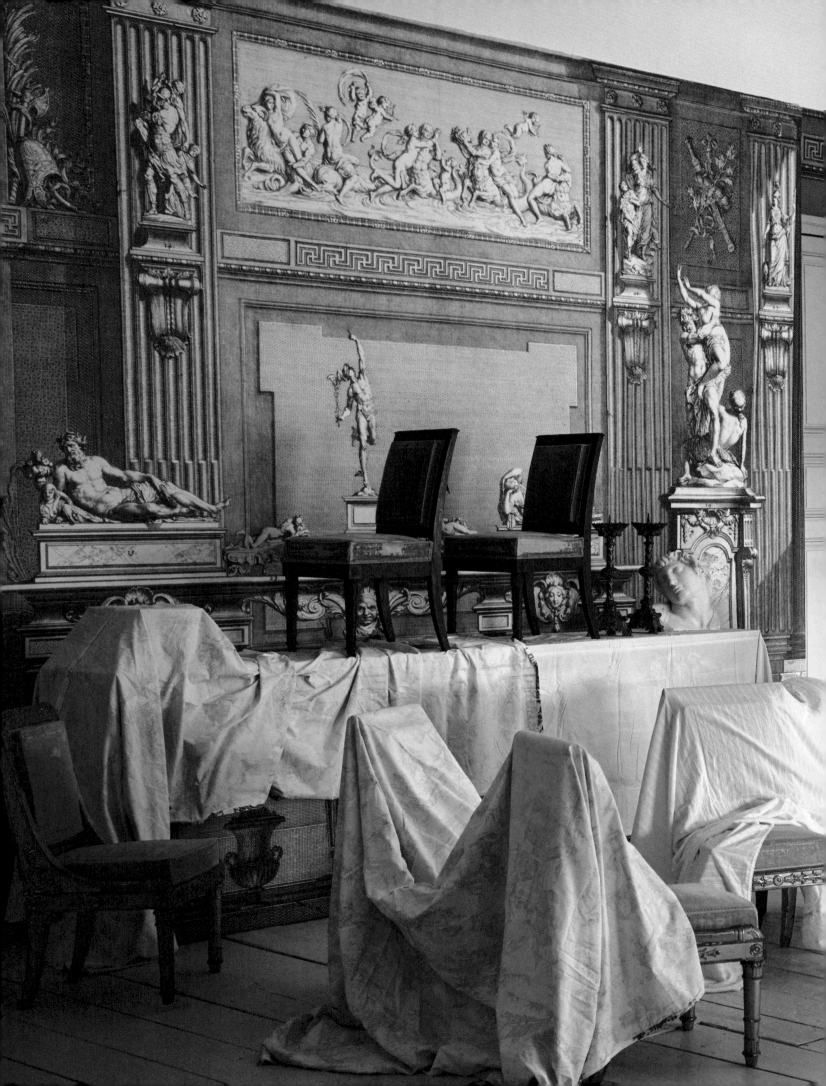

PRIVATE HAROUÉ

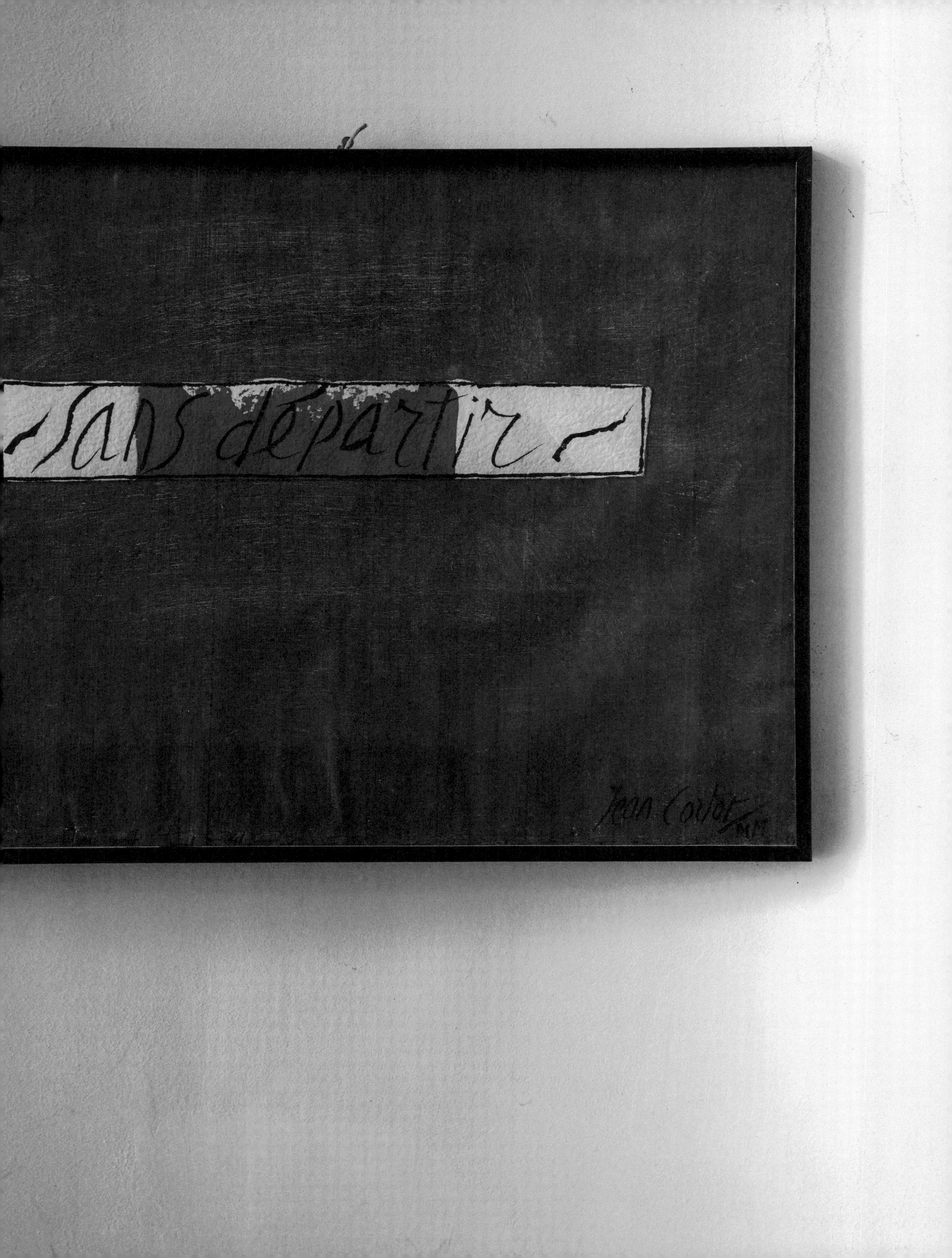
sans départir
Jean Cortot

HAROUÉ, FRENCH STYLE

Haroué is not just a historic monument—it is also a family home. "The west wing is where we live our daily life. It is not open to the public. This is where all the household muddle is, and where friends from all over the world congregate," Minnie explains. Conversation flows freely, dogs loll around on the couches, and everyone goes about their business.

Minnie made a hideaway for herself in one of the château's four towers. Here in her office, a cluster of photographs of her loved ones covers the mantelpiece. Above them hangs a wooden frame with all of the house keys hanging from it. A small painting in the family colors—red and yellow—catches the eye. It consists of the words *"Sans départir,"* the family motto, hand-written by the painter Jean Cortot. Meaning "never to forsake" and attributed to King René of Anjou (1409–1480), it is intended to indicate the strength of the Beauvau-Craon family's commitment to all those to whom it has pledged its loyalty.

Breakfast is taken in the small dining room lined with a floral fabric from the historic French manufacturer Le Manach. On the wall are a series of aquatints by Thomas Daniell and his nephew William, two English painters who went to immerse themselves in the exoticism of India and the light of the Far East in the nineteenth century. These were brought back by Giovanni Gregorini, the owner's great-uncle, testifying to the family's liking for long-distance travel, changes of scenery, and the discovery of other cultures.

In these private rooms, travel souvenirs stand side by side with precious ornaments and family pictures. Thus, in the small salon lined in ocher-colored velvet, you can admire an antique Cordoba leather paravent with bird and flower motifs that has been converted into a wall hanging. On one of the side tables are some hand-woven pots that Victoria and Sebastian, Minnie's children, brought back from their holidays in Cartagena, Colombia. They are made by the Wounaan community on the Pacific coast and are mixed with the house's "historic" ornaments. Elsewhere on the wall, in a gilded wooden frame, is a nineteenth-century picture that invites the visitor's gaze on the diversion of a walk through Pisa's Campo Santo, in the atmosphere of Renaissance Italy.

In the afternoon, after a long walk, in boots and warm sweaters, tea is taken in the library. Guests sit on deep couches—gifts from the late interior designer Alberto Pinto—with red as the dominant color, scattered with cushions embroidered by Princess Gabrielle d'Arenberg, Minnie's aunt. In crimson velvet with gold trim, they bear the names of the operas that have been performed during the Opéra en Plein Air events at the château: *Carmen*, *La Traviata*... In the evening, aperitifs are taken in a laid-back, convivial manner, while engaging in the art of witty and light-hearted conversation just

as it was done in the eighteenth century. There is no strict dress code, but rather a carefully devised, relaxed elegance. Velvet jackets and shawls are often appropriate. Sometimes a little cold draft makes the ladies shiver, and they gather around the fireplace. Minnie often wears a silk caftan embroidered with colorful motifs, which she brought back from her trips to India. The fire crackles in the Boffrand-designed fireplace. The room has an incredibly warm atmosphere, with its floor covered in a thick Persian carpet, its faded pink curtains, the ornaments, and the family portraits that bear witness to a long history. On occasional tables dressed with "cloths" of seventeenth-century Cordoba leather, Minnie places large bouquets of lilies—her favorite flowers—and the room fills with their fragrance, which so befits the library's opulence. Drinks are served casually: each guest can take what they want at the bar, which is covered in an oriental carpet. Some of the Beauvau-Craon family's history is displayed on the walls—ancestors keep watch! Between two windows is a portrait of the Duke of Choiseul, who led Louis XV's government. He wears silk stockings and shoes with red heels, the latter a sartorial detail that indicates he belonged to the highest level of aristocracy and recalls Roman sandals—a fashion that perhaps inspired the

famous shoe designer Christian Louboutin. In the middle of one wall is a large picture of Charles-Louis de Beauvau-Craon, Minnie's grandfather, born in 1878. He is portrayed as a child, along with his younger sister, Marie-Henriette, who is holding a doll dressed entirely in lace. Marie-Henriette was to become Charles d'Harcourt's wife and the owner of the Château du Champ-de-Bataille, which now belongs to the architect and designer Jacques Garcia.

A full-length portrait of King Louis XV, given by him to the Prince who built the château, presides over the Aleppo marble fireplace. This portrait is flanked by others depicting some of the first Prince's twenty children. Among them can be spotted Marshal Charles-Just de Beauvau-Craon and his wife. Hanging in the center of the room is a large Murano glass chandelier, installed there by Minnie's Italian grandmother.

The full length of the wall facing the windows is fitted with beautiful bookcases featuring carved Corinthian pilasters. These are the work of Germain Boffrand, who was also responsible for designing the château's fireplaces and trumeaux. The bookcases themselves contain a large number of historic volumes. Among them are Boccaccio's *Il Filostrato*—an epic poem on the Trojan War, which Louis de Beauvau was the first person to translate into French, in the fifteenth century—as well as the published letters of the Princess Palatine, a merciless letter-writer who recounted the goings-on at the Versailles court in intimate detail, and a much-consulted copy of Germain Boffrand's *Book of Architecture*. More recently, Maurice Barrès's *La Colline inspirée* has found its place here. Barrès was Minnie's father's godfather, along with Marshal Lyautey.

"La princesse est servie" (The Princess is served)—this little phrase is still in use, announced by Lucian, the family's very loyal butler, to let guests know that it is time to head for the dining room.

Here again the taste for travel is evident, through a large canvas representing a fantasia on Marco Polo's journeys in India. The oak wall paneling is ornamented with sections of Italian folding screens inset with decorative trompe-l'oeil panels that depict landscapes and urns overflowing with flowers. Here too, dinners more often than not take the form of a buffet, so that guests can serve themselves as they choose.

When Minnie holds a dinner with table service, the preparations follow more formal codes, to meet the demands of the French art of living. Minnie strives to bring a festive atmosphere to these soirees. The white tablecloth with its underlay, the silverware, the Baccarat crystal glasses and carafes, and the fine porcelain bearing the family crest are laid out. Dinners always being candle lit, the silver candelabras take centerpiece on the tables.

During formal dinners, a stand is placed at the door of the library leading to the dining room displaying the seating plan where guests can find their placement. For the dinner, Minnie cultivates an air of refined simplicity. Soufflés, poultry, and for dessert often a strawberry cream cake or baba au rhum—a nod to Stanisław, who invented it. After dinner, all retire to the library to have a cup of coffee or an herbal infusion around the crackling fire, relax on the couches, or savor an aged homemade mirabelle plum liqueur…

For more intimate dinners, Minnie has a round table set in the splendid west tower, next to the formal dinning room. Here, a colored tablecloth is often used. Minnie has a soft spot for the yellow malachite-effect tablecloth that brings light to the tower. Silver animal figures, unglazed Sèvres porcelain ornaments, or a bunch of roses from the garden placed in a silver cup serve as delightful centerpieces. From here, you can see the moat and swans, the gardens, the wooded area, the bridges, and the roofs of the Château Bassompierre. Time seems to stand still…

THE TAJE MAHEL, AGRA.

"I've never found an adjective that quite sums up Haroué. It's big, it's beautiful, it's… enormous! Haroué is a family home, but also a place that has been open to the public for decades.

Even though we don't live here—I live in Geneva with my family—hardly a day goes by without us saying the name Haroué. Haroué is a privilege that we must be conscious of.

I'm proud of Haroué, and of what my mother has done with it. The most important events of my personal life—like my wedding—happened here. There's the private Haroué, the one that I want to pass on to my daughter because it's our family's roots. It's our home, our identity. And then there's the public Haroué, the one we want to share."

—SEBASTIAN BOTANA DE BEAUVAU-CRAON

QUEEN MUM, AN UNFORGETTABLE WEEK

In May 1979, Queen Elizabeth, The Queen Mother, came to spend a week at Haroué. A portrait of her in evening dress, wearing a diamond diadem and a white fox stole, is a reminder of the event. It is the official court portrait, in a monogrammed silver frame, that she would send as a thank-you to hosts she had stayed with.

"The Queen Mother was the nicest and wittiest person you could imagine, she spoke fluent French. Her Majesty came with her three enormous Daimlers. Queen Mum was elegant and refined, and would match her jewelry to her outfits—sapphires, emeralds, or pearls, depending on the circumstances. She brought her serving staff, hairdresser, chauffeurs, chambermaid, and her own gin with her, as well as her cigarettes!" recalls Minnie who, along with her sister, Diane, their father, and his wife, Laure, had spent an unforgettable week.

A sufficiently large and grand house was required to accommodate The Queen Mother, who came to France between May and June every year with her friends and her ladies-in-waiting. Prince Jean-Louis de Faucigny-Lucinge, a friend of Marc de Beauvau-Craon, had suggested Haroué.

A close friend of The Queen Mother came with her, Lady Fermoy—Lady Diana's grandmother.

Odette Pol-Roger was also there. "Tante Odette was our stepmother Laure's godmother, and had been Churchill's muse during the war: he was dazzled by her. She was full of charm. Churchill always used to drink Pol Roger champagne in reminiscence of her," Minnie remembers.

A very special guest was also invited: Miss Baker, Minnie and Diane's English nanny. Thinking about her always makes Minnie emotional. That time was defined by both etiquette and simplicity. The English party had gently taken over the service in the château. Every evening, dinner was by candlelight in evening gowns and dinner jackets, and, after dinner, everyone would go and convene beside the grand fireplace, drinking gin or mirabelle liqueur—which The Queen Mother enjoyed—and chatting openly while playing cards. Sometimes Lady Fermoy would take to the piano. The soirees were relaxed and joyful. The Queen Mother was last to go to bed at night, but first to get up in the morning.

When the time came for them to leave, The Queen Mother—remembering that the Prince had told her about some treasure that had been hidden in the orchard during the war—presented him with a metal detector brought especially from England.

Minnie Duncan

8 Juin

1978

SALLE a MANGER

Madame Ortiz

Monsieur Aicardi

M. Duncan Mc Laren

Princesse de Polignac

Mademoiselle Minni
de Beauvau Craon

Prince
de Beauvau Craon

Monsieur Antenor Patino

Duchesse de la
Rochefoucauld

Madame Staunton

I

Comte de Guichen

Comtesse de Rougemont

Sir
James Goldsmith

Princesse
J. d. de
Broglie

Mr Gerald
Van der Kemp

Monsieur
George Ortiz

Lady Granard

Duchesse
Torlonia

Lord Granard

Madame
Van der Kemp

Marquis
de Casteja

Duc d'Harcourt

II

Madame Patino

Duc de La
Rochefoucauld

Madame Kristo
Kurteff

Princesse
de Beauvau Craon

Monsieur Staunton

III

Baron
de Waldner

Sir Valentine
Abdy

Madame Olivier Hoare

Duchesse d'Harcourt

Madame
Michel Sard Veil

Monsieur Loudon

GALERIE

Monsieur
Puzenat

Madame
Thaw

Madame Mattison

Prince Colonna

Comte de Rougemont

IV

Marquise de Casteja

Comtesse
di Marcello

Monsieur
Olivier Hoare

Baron Humbert des Lyons
de Feuchin

Madame Loudon

Monsieur Etchevarria

Lady Bixley

Graf
Trolle-Bonde

Madame
Jaime Ortiz
Patino

Madame
Puzenat

Duc Torlonia

Madame
Brignone

Baron Edouard
de l'Epée

Monsieur
Jaime Ortiz-Patino

Comtesse
di Rorasenda

Monsieur
Graham
Mattison

Madame Isabel
Goldsmith

Baronne
de Waldner

V

Monsieur
du Pasquier

VI

Mr Elie Schnaoui

Lady Abdy

Comte
de Nicolay

Raymond

Madame Elie
Schnaoui

Comte
Leonello Brandolini

Mademoiselle Sala

Monsieur Larivière

Mademoiselle
Cristina Schneider

Madame
George Ortiz

Baron
Roland de l'Epée

Prince de Poix

VII

Mademoiselle
Diane de Beauvau
Craon

Princesse
de Chimay

Monsieur Jean-François
Daigre

Monsieur Pierre
Maraval

Mademoiselle
Pilar Irisarri

GUEST ROOMS

When you go and spend a weekend at Haroué, you will be given one of the guest rooms. You will sleep in white Egyptian cotton sheets monogrammed with the family's coat of arms, kept warm by a bedcover in faded tones. Minnie and her children make sure guests feel comfortable by putting art books and novels in French, English, or Italian in each bedroom, as well as flowers from the garden. There is no formal coordination between the walls and fabrics, but just an array of glorious chintzes that make for a welcoming interior.

The rooms are like small suites: an antechamber, a bedroom, and a practical, understated, old-fashioned bathroom decorated with English engravings of horses or flowers. Most of the bedrooms have remained unchanged for a long time and retain the charm of grand historic houses.

The rooms make you feel at home from the very first moment. They have that slightly old-fashioned elegance of fine houses where objets d'art, pictures, flowers from the garden, and family souvenirs are all mingled together. Lined up along the wall in the small salon adjoining the bedroom of Marc de Beauvau-Craon, Haroué's last Prince, are large closets that contain a portion of the family archives. On a little side table is a fragment of Louis XVIII's coronation mantle, with fleurs-de-lys embroidered in gold thread on deep-purple velvet. The bedroom's walls are lined with a paisley-pattern fabric in tones of blue. A collection of small pictures by the painter Jean-Marc Winckler, a gift from the artist, depicts Haroué from different angles. In these, one can notice a group of cherubs by Guibal, and views of the château and countryside. Above the fireplace, a portrait of a Spanish young lady holding a *chocolatière* lends the

room a sense of sweetness. The furniture, made of elm and with swan's-neck features, is upholstered in the same fabric that lines the walls.

In another guest room, the antechamber's walls are hung with a flurry of Neapolitan engravings depicting minor trades. They are prettily framed in canvas fabric with a trompe-l'œil floral motif. This time the bedroom walls are covered with an indienne featuring voluptuous peonies, bringing a feeling of freshness to the room. The bed has a padded headboard and is covered in the same fabric as the walls. Here you can be assured of sweet dreams, watched over by three cherubs in a painting brought from Bologna by Minnie Gregorini-Bingham, the current owner's grandmother.

What could be more dazzling and feminine than the pink-and-orange chintz adorning the walls of Victoria's bedroom? A daybed upholstered in black-and-white toile de Jouy sits happily alongside the little parasol-carrying monkeys on the wall fabric. The woodwork and paneling is painted antique pink, making the room look even more joyful. To hide the cast-iron radiator that heats the space well when temperatures drop, Victoria has placed a small folding screen in front of it, featuring toile de Jouy with yellow motifs on a white ground. On the side table are a bunch of peonies and, in a silver frame, a portrait of Minnie and Javier, her parents.

In the long corridor from which the bedrooms are accessed, a series of low bookcases are filled with books gathered by successive generations of Haroué's residents. Art and architecture books rub shoulders with volumes on travel, novels, fashion magazines, and children's books, from Bécassine to Beatrix Potter and Jules Verne…

THE ATTICS

248
ELEGANT SIMPLICITY

ELEGANT SIMPLICITY

A vast space that possesses a raw, stripped-back sort of beauty, smells of wood, oozes grandeur, and is handsome and serene like a cathedral. It is by exploring these attics with their floor area of 1.4 hectares (3.5 acres) that you get a real sense of how imposing this "house" is. Large reinforced-concrete struts were installed in 1920, during the château's restoration by Minnie's grandparents. They support the eighteenth-century slate roof. The spaces are delineated by red-brick walls, with no doors to link them; there are pine floorboards throughout; and the balustrade of the staircase leading up to the attic of the house is also by Germain Boffrand.

The space is completely bare, without the slightest pretense, embracing the majestic architecture. The four towers are covered with a roof truss made of solid oak, fixed entirely with wooden pegs and using no metal whatsoever—the work of carpenters who have achieved the status of Compagnons du Devoir, preserving an age-old tradition. They repaired the tower and its roof structure after the great storm of the winter of 1999. That year, on December 26, the family were all together for a quiet Christmas when Cyclone Lothar tore away the slates from the west tower, which flew off one after another as the storm swept through the attics like an unstoppable whirlwind. In the morning, a frightening sight presented itself. Thanks to the expertise of the master craftsmen that are the Compagnons du Devoir, all trace of the destruction was erased and the attics now seem sturdier than ever. Each year, Minnie takes a "roof tour" with these specialists, led by the Chief Architect of Historic Monuments, to check that the covering is in good condition and to remedy any weather damage. Like all of France's listed Historic Monuments, the Château de Haroué receives some financial support from the Regional Cultural Affairs Directorate, and also from the Grand-Est region and the Meurthe-et-Moselle department.

Just underneath the attics are a series of small staff bedrooms. They are situated exactly above the apartments of the master and lady of the house, and of the guests to whom the staff members were "assigned." Some of these little bedrooms harbor treasures that trigger family memories—the riding boots that were made to measure for Victoria and Sebastian's grandfather, and traveling trunks, as well as children's toys, automata, dolls, and dollhouses that Minnie and Diane used to play with. In sun-bleached hatboxes slumber bowlers and top hats. The closets contain haute-couture dresses worn by Minnie Gregorini-Bingham, designed by Poiret, Madame Grès, and Jeanne Lanvin. This is the realm where, as children, Minnie and Diane used to dress up… as princesses!

CAPTIONS

Page 2: The château's entrance hall.

Pages 4–5: The main courtyard with its monumental gateway and railings designed by Jean Lamour.

Pages 6–7: One of the cellars.

Pages 8–9: Detail of the chinoiserie decor in the Pillement tower.

Pages 10–11: Detail of the ceiling in the Salon Hébert.

Pages 12–13: In the salon-library, the bookcases designed by Germain Boffrand.

Pages 14–15: A delightful jumble of fond memories stashed away for years… On the right, a pastel portrait of Princess Minnie aged eight. On the left, riding boots made to measure for Charles-Louis de Beauvau-Craon, Minnie's grandfather. The wallpaper dates from the 1920s.

Page 16: Saint Sebastian.

Page 18: Window overlooking the pedimented entrance in the main courtyard.

Page 20: Princess Minnie de Beauvau-Craon in the Alexander Salon, in front of one of the tapestries.

Page 23: Princess Minnie de Beauvau-Craon on the drawbridge.

Page 25: Part of the stair railing by Jean Lamour: the Beauvau-Craon family's cipher of interwoven letter Cs of the family name.

ARCHITECTURE AND GARDENS

Page 26: Heart-shaped padlock by Jean Lamour.

Pages 30–31: Plan of the "green carpet" garden by Emilio Terry.

Pages 34–35: A "palace in the fields," looming up from the gentle Lorraine countryside.

Page 36: Moat swans…

Page 37: An alley through the grove of trees.

Pages 38–39: Haroué's rear facade. The writer Maurice Barrès considered it the "finest château… fully intact" and wanted the Prince of Beauvau-Craon to return here.

Pages 40–41: In the gardens, designed *à la française*, on the left is a stone statue representing *Winter*. On the right, *Autumn*. Both are attributed to the sculptor Barthélemy Guibal.

Pages 42–43: Detail of Emilio Terry's French-style gardens, with hornbeams trimmed into alternating conical and trapezoid shapes.

Pages 44–45: The Lorraine landscape and the typically French gardens.

Page 46: The drawbridge at sunset.

Page 47: A cherub by Barthélemy Guibal holding the Constable of Lorraine's sword.

Page 48: The Bassompierre gate seen from the château's east tower.

Page 49: The still waters of the moat, on the east side.

Page 51: A quiet moment beneath the trees for Victoria and Winnie…

Pages 52–53: The tack room, unchanged over the centuries.

Page 54: In the stables, wonderful seventeenth-century paving made of bricks arranged like a piece of marquetry, bearing the patina of time.

Page 55: The tack room.

Pages 56–57: Beyond the stone wall that surrounds the château's grounds, a glimpse of the orchard and Haroué's slate-covered towers soaring toward the sky.

Page 58: Intact pigeonholes in the dovecote. The number of these indicated the owner's wealth.

Page 59: View of the dovecote and the English-style garden.

Pages 60–61: Haroué looking majestic yet mellow, at the end of a summer's day…

Pages 62–63: Chestnut trees several hundred years old, like operatic curtains framing the stage of the main courtyard.

Pages 64–65: The stone pediment above the main entrance is the work of Barthélemy Guibal. It features the Beauvau-Craon coat of arms flanked by angels, and with the crown of the Princes of the Holy Roman Empire in its apex.

Page 66: Entrance to the family vault, surmounted by its coat of arms.

Page 67: One of the main courtyard's two arcades.

Pages 68–69: The château's chapel. On the wall, tapestries featuring the Beauvau-Craon lion rampant flank the sculpted altar by César Bagard.

Page 70: Prie-dieu embroidered in petit point by the grandmother of the château's owner, also named Minnie de Beauvau-Craon.

Page 71: The chapel's austere benches, with engravings by Leonardo da Vinci above.

Page 154: A billiard settee from the collection, watched over by the young Louis XVI and Louis XVIII.

Page 155: The mahogany armchairs in the billiard room, with armrests in the form of winged griffin heads, lined up as if on parade.

Pages 156–157: The grand Louis XVIII salon, designed by the École Boulle, on the first floor. The beautiful forty-eight-light Baccarat chandelier was presented by the Lorraine-based crystal firm as a gift in 1998.

Pages 158–159: Miniatures, tiepins, seals, and ornaments belonging to the family. In the center, a subtle portrait of Minnie Gregorini-Bingham, the current owner's grandmother.

Page 160: A half-open door offers a glimpse of the Givenchy salon's grisaille decor.

Page 161: Detail of the Aubusson carpet.

Page 162–163: The royal furniture in the Givenchy salon, protected by sheets.

Pages 164–165–166: The antechamber that leads through to the Louis XVIII salon. The walls are covered in wallpaper with a fleur-de-lys design bought by the Princess at the Drouot auction house. Eighteenth-century Austrian stove.

Page 167: Grisaille portrait of King Louis XVIII.

Pages 168–169: The so-called "Louis XVIII" bedroom with its full set of furniture. Bed, bedside tables, and cheval mirror, all in mahogany and bronze. On the walls, a collection of grisaille engravings representing the signs of the zodiac.

PRIVATE HAROUÉ

Page 170: The entrance to Haroué's private apartments. On the wall, an antique plan of Bologna, the city where the current owner's grandmother Minnie Gregorini-Bingham was born. On the chest, a small antique trunk made of leather.

Page 172: Minnie's office, painted in yellow like a sunflower.

Page 173: *"Sans départir"* ("Never to forsake"), the Beauvau-Craon family's motto, painted by Jean Cortot.

Page 175: The latchkey with a Little Prince key ring.

Page 178: A mirror in the entrance lobby, with a reflection of the château's main courtyard.

Page 179: Ground-floor passage with stone flooring, leading to the guest bedrooms. Between the windows are two nineteenth-century wood chests.

Page 180: The Prince's winter overcoat.

Page 181: Pepito and Loukhoum, guardians of the castle.

Pages 182–183: The dining room table set for breakfast. On the wall is a large canvas depicting Marco Polo's voyages. On the ceiling, a nine-light Empire-period chandelier.

Pages 184–185: The dining room walls are hung with Le Manach floral fabric. On the wall are aquatints by Thomas and William Daniell depicting their travels in India. In the alcove, a large Godin stove gently heats the space.

Page 186: Purity of forms: a single bronze candlestick stands alongside an obelisk.

Page 187: In the small salon with velvet-covered walls, souvenirs from the family's travels have accumulated over the years. On the occasional table, Colombian hand-woven baskets brought back by Victoria and Sebastian.

Pages 188–189: The small salon's warm decor. On the left, detail of the Cordoba leather folding screen that has been altered to hang as a picture. In front of this, the occasional table where the Colombian hand-woven baskets sit. On the right, a nineteenth-century painting of the Campo Santo in Pisa hangs on the wall.

Page 190: The enfilade viewed from the salon-library.

Page 191: Detail of the salon-library.

Pages 192–193: The large salon-library by Germain Boffrand is the heart of the château. Couches by Alberto Pinto. Murano glass chandelier. Above the fireplace, a portrait of Louis XV that was a gift to Prince Marc de Beauvau-Craon, who built the château.

Page 195: Sebastian, Lavinia, and their daughter, Isabella, in front of the bookcases.

Page 196: Books in the salon-library bearing heraldic devices record the family's history.

Page 197: Detail of ornaments on a table covered with a Cordoba leather "cloth," in the salon-library.

Page 199: Portrait of the Duke of Choiseul in a vermilion velvet outfit. Placed on the marble top of the chest of drawers, a souvenir photo of Queen Elizabeth, The Queen Mother, and on the left a porcelain cameo of Stanislas, Chevalier de Boufflers.

Pages 200–201: The salon-library with its warm atmosphere. Aperitifs are taken here before dinner, under the watchful eyes of Charles-Louis de Beauvau-Craon and his sister Marie-Henriette, depicted as children.

Page 202: Table plan for Minnie's engagement dinner in 1978, by the Russian painter and decorator Alexandre Serebriakoff (1907–1995).

Page 203: Snuffer held aloft by Hermes, the god of travel.

Pages 204–205: Marco Polo's voyages again, in the main dining room.

Pages 206–207: The canteen of grand silverware… guarded by Loukhoum.

Pages 208–209: Preparations for a dinner with table service.

Page 210: Detailed examination of the silverware before a grand dinner.

Page 211: Tableware bearing the cipher of Louis-Philippe, King of France from 1830 to 1848.

Pages 212–213: The table all set.

Page 214: Rack of lamb Champvallon.

Page 215: Detail of a table set for dinner: the Sèvres porcelain dinner plates bear Louis-Philippe's cipher, the cutlery is vermeil, and the glasses are the Harcourt design, in Baccarat crystal.

Pages 216–217: Chinese porcelain for a strawberry charlotte.

Page 218: A linen napkin discarded on a Bellanger mahogany dining chair.

Page 219: At the end of the meal, the guests have just left the table.

Page 221: Pools of light flood into the upstairs level of the west wing. Corridor and staircase by Germain Boffrand.

Pages 222–223: Pepito holds the fort in the archive room.

Page 224: Placed on a games table, a photo of Prince Marc de Beauvau-Craon; behind, a fragment of the fabric from Louis XVIII's coronation mantle.

Page 225: In the archive room, two nineteenth-century fireside chairs and a collection of walking sticks.

Pages 226–227: Guest bedroom with swan's-neck furniture. Above the fireplace is a Spanish portrait of a woman holding a *chocolatière*. Architectural drawings mingle with pictures by Jean-Marc Winckler above the pale wood chest of drawers.

Pages 228–229: The anteroom of a guest suite. On the table with its broad cloth, a few peonies from the garden are arranged in a deep-blue Sèvres porcelain vase. The walls are lined with paisley-print fabric by Pierre Frey. A Persian carpet extends across the black-and-white checkerboard stone flooring.

Pages 230–231: No comment.

Page 232: Where's Andy?

Page 233: Another guest bedroom, brightly decorated. In the antechamber are Neapolitan engravings representing daily life scenes.

Pages 234–235: The bed's headboard is upholstered in the same floral fabric that covers the walls.

Page 236: In the boudoir: dresses by Philippe Venet.

Page 237: The charm of a bathroom.

Pages 238–239: Silver toilet accessories bearing the Beauvau-Craon coat of arms, in a case lined in oxblood-colored crushed velvet.

Page 240: Victoria's bedroom is decorated in ocher and orange, cheerful and bright. In the foreground, a daybed covered in black-and-white toile de Jouy echoes the themes portrayed on the exotic fabric that lines the walls.

Page 241: A photo of Victoria's parents, Minnie and Javier, in a silver frame. The peonies are from the "English" garden.

Page 242: A fine silk curtain stirred by a gust of wind…

Page 243: A family portrait set against a background of floral chintz in a guest bedroom.

Page 244: A jumble of books from one of the bookcases.

Page 245: A staircase in the west wing that leads to the guest bedrooms corridor.

THE ATTICS

Page 246: One of the small bedrooms just beneath the attic space.

Page 249: The oak staircase by Germain Boffrand, intact, which leads to the attics.

Page 250: A former bedroom beneath the attics.

Page 251: Corridor leading to the attics.

Pages 252–253: The unrestored east tower.

Page 254: Various objects are stored away in the attics. A toy stove on the right, together with two comfortable armchairs, paneling that awaits a new destination, and two pairs of skis from the 1960s.

Page 255: A mystery in the attics. Work never completed on this space directly above the Givenchy salon.

Pages 256–257: In the attics, the solid red brick walls.and the pine boards that cover the entire floor on this level are left bare.

Pages 258–259: Minnie gazes dreamily at the majestic roof structure.

Pages 260–261: A magnificent roof truss, fixed entirely with wooden pegs.

Page 262: Inside the east tower, which lost its roof in Cyclone Lothar in December 1999. It has been restored by the Compagnons du Devoir.

Page 263: Iron bracing.

Page 265: "Please close the door." Thank you!

Page 270: A tender moment shared by Minnie and Victoria on the balcony.

ACKNOWLEDGMENTS

MINNIE, VICTORIA, AND SEBASTIAN WOULD LIKE TO THANK:

For bringing this book into being:
Miguel Flores-Vianna, who believed in the project from day one and offers such a glorious vision of Haroué through his camera lens; Peter Copping for so marvelously making the house look its best; Jonathan Christie for designing the book so beautifully; Erik Winterstam for his great sensitivity and attentiveness; Monique Raux, who was so crucial to the writing of the text, her husband, Alain Gérin, for his unfailing friendship, and their daughter Nima; Jean-Louis Deniot for such an elegant and apt preface; the publishers, Catherine Bonifassi, her daughter, Louise, and the wonderful team at Cassi Édition; Charles Miers, publisher at Rizzoli New York, who enabled this book to take shape. Johann Chauvin, the chef; Marianne Guedin for her beautiful flowers.

The businesses and individuals who have contributed to enhancing the château's beauty over the years:
The chief architects of the Monuments Historiques, especially Pierre Colas and Pierre-Yves Caillault; our longstanding friend the architect Guillaume Pellerin, whose guidance we painfully miss; Philippe Vidal, President of the SNVB-CIC bank, the primary sponsor that made it possible for us to undertake the work on the first floor containing the private apartments; Thierry France-Lanord and the France-Lanord & Bichaton firm; the Compagnons du Devoir and the Coanus firm; Brice Guelorget and his magic aerial bucket truck; the Friends of the Château de Haroué association, its first president, Chantal Heimendinger, and her husband, Jean Heimendinger, without whom the work on that first floor would not have happened, and later president, Bérangère de Beco; Professor François Pupil, who enabled the École Boulle to come to the château; the students of the École Boulle.

For their role in promoting the château:
Roselyne Bachelot, Minister of Culture; Frédéric Mitterrand, former Minister of Culture. The Prefects of Meurthe-et-Moselle, especially Claude Érignac and Éric Freysselinard. Jean Rottner, President of the Grand-Est region; Jean-Luc Bohl, Vice-President of the Grand-Est region; Pascal Mangin, Grand-Est Regional Councillor and President of the region's Culture Commission. Valérie Beausert-Leick, President of the Departmental Council of Meurthe-et-Moselle, and her predecessors, especially Claude Huriet, Michel Dinet; Nicole Creusot, Vice-President of the Departmental Council of Meurthe-et-Moselle; Jean-François Husson, Senator of Meurthe-et-Moselle. Mathieu Klein, Mayor of Nancy; Jean-Baptiste de Froment, special adviser to the Minister of Culture. Daniel Alcouffe, Chief Curator at the Musée du Louvre. Stéphane Bern, impassioned defender of heritage and Haroué, a steadfast family friend. Gérard Longuet, former Minister, Senator of the Meuse, for his ever-faithful friendship and support. Alain Marais, Regional Director of Cultural Affairs, who has been so supportive to us. Daniel Rondeau, former ambassador, member of the Académie Française, and his wife, Noëlle Rondeau, for their friendship. Philippe Bélaval, President of the Centre des Monuments Nationaux, and his colleagues, who have enabled Haroué to embark upon a new chapter in its marvelous story. Jean-Marc Bouré, director of the Palais du Tau in Reims and the Château de Haroué. Alain Missoffe, whose valuable advice has always guided us; Françoise de Panafieu for her crucial support; Caroline Pigozzi, our longstanding friend.

The residents and mayors of Haroué, and a warm tribute to all who have visited us from Lorraine, France, and elsewhere, as well as those we look forward to welcoming in future.

For their warmth and friendship:
Her Serene Highness Princess A. d'Arenberg, Nandana Basnayakage, Diane de Beauvau-Craon, Yunes de Beauvau-Craon, Véronique Benitah, Christophe Bolloré, Javier Botana, Lavinia Botana de Beauvau-Craon, Albina du Boisrouvray, Charlie Cator, Timothée Dufour, Tristan Duval, Hubert de Givenchy, Gala Gordon, Jean d'Haussonville, Patricia Heim, Anneliese Heinzelmann, William Holloway, Jean de Lambertye, Patrick Legant, Danielle Leheu, Lucian Livera, Jean Loyrette, Sarah Kasha, Stefano Migliore, Henri and Catherine de Mitry, Albéric de Montgolfier, Morgane Parmentier, Alexis and Loreley Picourt, Alberto Pinto, Frédéric Plancard, Anne-Marie Quenette, Rambert Rigaud, Bruno Roy, Daniel Rueda-Sandoval, Denis Schaming, Cristina Schneider, Elaine Sciolino, Jean-Guillaume de Tocqueville, Philippe Venet, Francis Vauthier, François and Christel de Wendel.

Château de Haroué: The Home of the Princes de Beauvau-Craon
A Great French Estate, A Family Home

First published in the United States of America in 2021 by
Rizzoli International Publications, Inc.
300 Park Avenue South
New York, NY 10010
www.rizzoliusa.com

Edited by Victoria Botana de Beauvau-Craon
Foreword by Jean-Louis Deniot
Text by Minnie de Beauvau-Craon and Monique Raux

Photography by Miguel Flores-Vianna
Page 78: © Anton Bea

Publisher: Charles Miers
Editorial Director: Catherine Bonifassi
Creative Direction: Peter Copping
Editor: Victorine Lamothe
Production Director: Maria Pia Gramaglia
Production Manager: Kaija Markoe
Managing Editor: Lynn Scrabis

Editorial Coordination:
CASSI EDITION
Vanessa Blondel, Valentine Ferrante, Abigail Grater

ISBN: 978-0-8478-7092-9
Library of Congress Control Number: 2021934561
2021 2022 2023 2024 / 10 9 8 7 6 5 4 3 2 1
Printed in Italy

Visit us online:
Facebook.com/RizzoliNewYork
Twitter: @Rizzoli_Books
Instagram.com/RizzoliBooks
Pinterest.com/RizzoliBooks
Youtube.com/RizzoliNY
Issuu.com/Rizzoli